Learning to Pray

EVAN PILKINGTON

Foreword by Kenneth Leech

Barbara,

With love from

Evan Pilkington.

Whitsunday 1987

Darton Longman and Todd
London

First published in 1986 by
Darton Longman and Todd Ltd
89 Lillie Road, London SW6 1UD

© Evan Pilkington 1986

ISBN 0 232 51702 9

British Library Cataloguing in Publication Data
Pilkington, Evan
  Learning to pray.
  1. Prayer
  I. Title
  248.3'2   BV215

ISBN 0–232–51702–9

Phototypeset by Input Typesetting Ltd, London SW19 8DR
Printed in Great Britain by
Anchor Brendon Ltd
Tiptree, Essex

To my family

Contents

Acknowledgements

I should like to acknowledge my debt to the many people who have taught and encouraged me to pray over the years – by what they wrote or what they said or what they were – especially Eric Abbott and Reginald Somerset-Ward.

I should also like to thank my wife, Puck, not only for typing the manuscript of this book, but for making valuable suggestions and criticisms in her own inimitable way.

Foreword

There is at the present time a great interest in what is called 'spirituality'. But this interest does not necessarily mean that people are more spiritual, that there is deeper encounter with the Spirit of God. Christians believe that at the heart of any authentic spiritual life there is the work of prayer. Yet a lot of talk about spirituality and the spiritual life is a way of avoiding this basic work of praying. We discuss prayer, read, or even write, books about it, listen to cassettes, attend talks and lectures. But all this activity can become yet another diversion, an escape, a protection from the central reality of the spiritual journey: the encounter with the living and true God.

Throughout his ministry, Evan Pilkington has been a wise and practical guide to many people in their quest to know and love God. This equally wise and practical book comes out of a long and deep experience as a spiritual director and pastor, and it will be a cause of great thankfulness among those of us to whom he has ministered that he has put some of this experience on paper. Of course, no book can be a substitute either for the relationship with God which is the heart of prayer, or for the personal guidance of a brother or sister in Christ who prays with us and for us. Yet there is a real need for a simple book on prayer which does not take too much for granted.

Here is such a simple and deeply practical book, one which deals with the areas which are often neglected. Many writers simply assume that their readers know what to do, and so much basic advice is left out. In this book, attention is given to the common difficulties which we all face, and to those well-tried disciplines and methods which support the life of prayer and enable it to flourish.

The great value of this book is that it is not seen as an end, but as a means to an end: that end is to help the reader to put the book aside and move into prayer. In this age of spiritual impoverishment I believe that many people will find Evan Pilkington's book a real help in their search for a 'closer walk with God'.

KENNETH LEECH

1

Why Should I Pray?

The object of the exercise

To begin at the beginning. Why should I pray? I pray in order to express my faith in God.

For one reason or another, I have said 'Yes' to God. Perhaps I have thought about it and decided that there is more to be said in favour of God than against. Or I was brought up to believe. Or I want to find a meaning to life. Or maybe I have a sense of mystery, a feeling that more goes on than meets the eye, that there is another dimension to life beyond what I can see and hear, weigh and measure. Or as the result of some spiritual experience. Anyhow, for one reason or another, I have burnt my boats, jumped into the water and cried 'I believe in God'. Or, to change the metaphor, I have come off the fence on the positive side. I am neither an atheist nor an agnostic. I am a believer, however hesitant, tentative and riddled with doubts.

In the seventeenth century, Pascal described this initial act of faith as a wager, a bet. In the nineteenth century, Kierkegaard described it as a leap, a jump. Well, I have placed my bet, I have made my jump. And now I pray. Because to pray is to communicate with God in whom I say 'I believe'. To pray is to practise my faith.

Ramakrishna was an Indian religious genius of the nineteenth century. In his book *Ramakrishna and his Disciples* Christopher Isherwood tells the story of two men, an agnostic doctor and a businessman, who went to see Ramakrishna out of curiosity. They expected to meet a freak and probably a fake, but they were charmed by his ordinariness and his friendliness and they stayed with him all one afternoon. 'Does God really exist?'

1

asked the doctor. 'Of course he exists,' said Ramakrishna. 'You don't see the stars in daytime, but that doesn't mean that they don't exist. There's butter in milk, but how could anyone guess that by looking at it? To get the butter you must churn the milk in a cool place. To get the vision of God you must practise mental disciplines – you can't see him just by wishing.'

It is not enough for me merely to 'believe in God'. I want to know God, 'to get the vision of God'. I want God to become a reality. But how? How do I discover another country; get to know another person? By living there; by spending time with the person. Prayer is spending time with God, living a spiritual life, practising 'mental disciplines'. That is how I discover God and get to know him. Prayer is a voyage of discovery.

Why should I pray? I pray in order to express my love of God.

As a Christian, I take my cue about God from what I see in Christ. And what do I see? Looking through Jesus, as through a tiny window into a large room, what do I see about the nature and character of God? That here is no all-powerful, capricious, tyrannical despot, ordering the world according to his whims and fancies. Here is no cold, disapproving, implacable judge, weighing our merits and dishing out rewards and punishments as he thinks fit. Here is no universal provider who is a bit touchy and won't give us anything unless we ask nicely, go down on our knees and grovel, sit up and beg like an obedient dog. No, here is a God who loves and who calls out our love in response, a God who attracts.

Mind you, this love is not a mere smiling, tolerant benevolence. Jesus was not 'gentle Jesus, meek and mild'. He was often very angry. He was the friend of people in need, the friend of the helpless, the hopeless, the loveless. The friend of the despised, disreputable deviants of society – the 'tax-collectors and sinners' of the Gospels. But he was the enemy of the self-satisfied, the closed-minded, the hard-hearted. The enemy of the hypocritical who hid their selfishness, greed and injustice under a cloak of respectability and a strict observance of religion. The enemy of double-think and double-talk. His anger was an attempt to shock them out of their complacency and their self-delusion, to rescue them from the evil which blinded them. No wonder they resisted, rejected and finally crucified him. He was a danger to their security. Yet on the cross his love still held. All that love could do now, unable to lift a hand or move a foot, was to pray. And that, according to St Luke's Gospel, is what Jesus did. He prayed for those who had crucified him. 'And Jesus said, Father forgive them, for they know not what they do.'

> High and lifted up, I see him on the eternal Calvary,
> And two piercèd hands are stretching east and west o'er
>   land and sea.
> On my knees I fall and worship that great Cross that shines
>   above,
> For the very God of Heaven is not Power, but Power of
>   Love.
>
> G. A. Studdert-Kennedy

This may seem a revolutionary view of God. But it is the Christian faith. It is the meaning and message of the incarnation. Meister Eckhart puts it beautifully in one of his sermons, preached in the fourteenth century:

> The greatest good God ever did for man was that he became man himself. Here I shall tell you a story that is relevant to this. There was once a rich man and a rich lady. The lady had an accident and lost one eye, at which she grieved exceedingly. Then the lord came to her and said, 'Wife, why are you so distressed? You should not be so distressed at losing your eye.' She said, 'Sir, I do not mourn because I have lost my eye, I mourn for fear you might love me the less.' Then he said, 'Lady, I love you.' Not long afterwards he put out one of his own eyes, and going to his wife, he said, 'Lady, so you may know I love you I have made myself like you; now I too have only one eye.' This is like man, who could scarcely believe that God loved him so much, until God put out one of his own eyes and assumed human nature.

In his life and death and resurrection, Jesus reveals God as being pure, unlimited, unbreakable love, a love which is finally victorious over both sin and death.

'We love him because he first loved us.' I do not have to earn the love of God, to deserve it by my good works, like the elder brother in the Parable of the Prodigal Son. The love of God is a free gift. All I have to do is to receive it in faith and to respond to it in love.

Elizabeth Barratt wrote to Robert Browning before they were married:

> If thou must love me, let it be for naught
> Except for love's sake only.

That is what God says to us in Christ. And so I pray

> Not for the sake of gaining aught,
> Not seeking a reward;
> But as thyself has lovèd me,
> O ever-loving Lord.

This, perhaps, is the distinctive thing about Christian prayer, its motivation. It is a love relationship. It is the response of love to Love. As Meister Eckhart put it, 'that which embraces is that which is embraced'. I do not pray in order to get something out of God. I pray in order to give something to God. My prayer is the gift of my love in response to his amazing, unbelievable love revealed in Christ.

Why should I pray? I pray in order that I may be open to God. God is not like a possessive parent, always interfering, never allowing me to be myself, to make my own decisions. God leaves me free. He waits to be asked. I have to open the door and invite him in. 'Behold, I stand at the door and knock; if anyone hears my voice and opens the door, I will come in to him and eat with him and he with me.'

When I pray, I open the doors of my life to God and let him in. And he comes in. He comes in to purify and to transform my life. He cleans the place up a bit, moving the furniture around and throwing some of it out. He cleans the windows, so that I can see other people and the world outside more clearly. He stocks the fridge and the deep-freeze with food to keep me going. He takes my temperature, puts me to bed and prescribes medicines to make me better. He ticks me off and cheers me up according to my need. That, of course, is picture language. But I hope you see what I mean. The presence of God judges, purifies, feeds, heals and strengthens me.

When I pray, I am exposed to God like a sunbather exposed to the sun. I am open to his grace – his gracious influence, his inflowing light and life and love and power.

Why should I pray? I pray in order to co-operate with God.

St Paul wrote to the Christians in Corinth that we are – or should be – 'workers together with him'. God leaves us free, either to co-operate with his purpose or to frustrate it. If I believe in God and if I desire to love him in response to his love revealed in Christ, I shall naturally want to work with him, not against him. To do his will, not my own; to follow his way, not mine. When I pray, I surrender my will to his. I express my desire to work 'together with him'. I offer myself as an instrument, a tool for him to use.

But prayer is not an individualistic thing – me and my God. 'No man is an Island', wrote John Donne, 'entire of itself, every man is a piece of the Continent, a part of the Main . . . I am involved with Mankind.' So other people will come into my prayer. The world will come into my prayer. And the Church in the world. When I pray, I offer myself as a channel through which the light and love and power of God can flow through into other people, into the world, into the Church.

Prayer is not escapism, 'the opium of the people'. When I pray, I am not escaping from the pressures of life, the irritations of other people, the problems and needs of the world, into a pious fantasy world above the bright blue sky. For God is Creator of the world. God is 'our Father'. God is love. When I pray, I am open and exposed to the all-embracing love of God. This should lead to an openness and responsiveness to life, to the world, to other people. And if it doesn't, that is a judgement upon my prayer – that it is self-centred, not God-centred. Kierkegaard has an image of two doors which open

5

and close together. Open the door onto God and you automatically open the door onto your neighbour. Close the door onto your neighbour and you automatically close the door onto God.

When I pray, I am not escaping from life. I am entering more fully into life. And my prayer should bear fruit in my life. Jesus said, 'By their fruits you shall know them.' That is the acid test of prayer.

2

When and Where shall I Pray?

Preparing for the journey

Prayer is a very strange activity. It is an attempt to communicate with a Being who is not accessible to our ordinary senses. We cannot see him, hear him, touch him, taste him. We cannot know God in the same way that we know another person. And yet we believe in him. We believe that he is real and we believe that he is personal in the sense that we *can* communicate with him and he with us. We possess a spiritual faculty deep down which can penetrate and be receptive to mystery. Our spirit can be open to the Spirit of God. But because it is strange, we should expect prayer to be difficult. And it is. We need all the practical help we can get.

Prayer requires discipline. You can't get anywhere in prayer without it. By discipline I mean making a plan, offering to God so many minutes of your time each day for this strange activity. This is called a Rule of Prayer. But do remember that a Rule of Prayer is meant to be a help, not a burden. It is not an ideal which you try to reach, a ladder which you have to climb. It is an anchor to hold you, to prevent you from drifting. So your rule must be a minimum thing, something which is well within your capacity. You can always do more than your rule promises, but never less. That is the point.

Father Andrew, who was a wise teacher of prayer, once said: 'Prayer is you praying.' It is not something exterior to you, like putting on a coat or wearing a hat. Prayer is *you* praying. And so the state of *you* at any given time will affect your prayer. I don't mean moods and inclinations, I mean circumstances. There are certain circumstances which alter, limit and restrict your ordinary life; for example, overstrain, illness and those

7

interruptions like moving house or having someone to stay. In such circumstances, you may well have to limit and adapt your Rule of Prayer. We must be humble and accept our limitations. God is not a hard taskmaster and we must not be scrupulous slaves. 'Circumstances alter cases', wrote St Thomas Aquinas. You can apply that ethical maxim to your Rule of Prayer. A useful yardstick as to whether you are able to pray properly is whether you can read a fairly serious book. Both require roughly the same amount of concentration. Neither overdriving yourself on the one hand, nor being overindulgent with yourself on the other – these are the twin dangers to avoid. Discipline and humility, humility and discipline.

It is a good thing to have a spiritual book on the go to feed your prayer. What sort of book? It must be a book which 'clicks' with you personally, a book you feel at home with like a wise and trusted friend, a book which speaks to your condition. People are always recommending books to us. 'You must read so and so, you must read such and such.' By all means have a look at them, have a quick browse through, but unless the recommended book 'clicks' with you, forget it. It is not the book for you now. It may be one day, but not now. We are all made differently, we all have different needs and we are all at different stages on the road. Choose your own book and read it slowly, a little at a time, pausing to think about it, to chew it over, to take it in. (Just for interest, I have included at the end of this book a list of some classic books of spiritual reading, with the names of the publishers. There are, of course, many other such books. My list is bound to be subjective – books which have helped me personally and other people whom I know.)

Now for the practicalities.

When shall I pray?

Don't say, 'I can pray any time', because in practice 'any time' can so easily become 'no time'. You need to tie yourself down, to fix a time. When shall that time be? This is a personal question and a personal decision. There isn't a right or a wrong time to pray. There is only the right time for you in your particular circumstances, with your particular timetable.

Think about it – what would be the best time for you? Before breakfast and the whirl of the day begins? After breakfast? Midmorning? During the lunch break if you are out at work? When you get home? Early evening? Only you can decide – by trial and error. What works best for you? The only thing to avoid is leaving it until too late in the day. Because, as I said, prayer demands considerable concentration and by the end of the day our concentration battery has run down. You can't really pray when you are tired.

Where shall I pray?

Again, don't say, 'I can pray anywhere', because in practice 'anywhere' can so easily become 'nowhere'. So choose the best place for you. Where shall it be? Where you can be alone and free from interruption. Jesus said, '. . . when you pray, go into your room and *shut the door*'.

Some people are more susceptible to atmosphere than others. Some people like to pray in a church, if possible, because it carries a spiritual atmosphere. Some people are helped by having visual aids around – a crucifix, an ikon, a picture, or just a bowl of flowers. Some people are helped by aural aids – listening to a piece of music which lifts the mind and heart to God. Some people are helped by physical aids – touching the beads of a rosary which they hold in their hands.

Think about it and choose the best place for you to pray, whether a church or a particular room. And surround yourself with whatever helps you to get in the mood, so to speak, whatever helps you to concentrate on what you are doing.

3

How Shall I Pray?

Setting out and finding my way

How shall I pray?

There is no right or wrong position for prayer. There is only the right physical position for you, where you can be relaxed and able to concentrate. You don't have to kneel down. You can quite happily sit in a chair, so long as it is not so comfortable that it makes you go to sleep! Or, if you do yoga, as many people do nowadays, you can take up a yoga position.

Always begin by getting still. That is vital. We come to our time of prayer with our body all tense and our mind racing. You can't pray in that state. You need, first of all, deliberately to relax your body, to unwind, and to let your mind quieten down.

There is a verse in one of the Psalms which says, 'Be still then, and know that I am God.' Begin with that.

Say '*Be still*' first of all to your body until, bit by bit, your muscles begin to relax and your breathing becomes slower and deeper. Then say the same words to your mind until, bit by bit, your mind begins to quieten down. Finally, say the same two words to your spirit, to you deep down, until you begin to let go and sink peacefully into the silence.

Then continue with the rest of that verse from the Psalm, taking it slowly, one word at a time.

'Be still then, *and know*.' Just 'know', know deep down, know for yourself, without inquiring exactly who or what or why you know. Two quotations may help here. The first is from a spiritual classic of the fourteenth century called *The Cloud of Unknowing*: 'Be willing to be blind, and give up all longing to know the why and how . . . It is enough that you should feel moved lovingly by you know not what, and that in this inward urge you have no real thought for anything less than God and that your desire is steadily and simply turned towards him.' The second is a sentence from a great German theologian of this century, Karl Barth: 'To know God means to stand in awe of him and to be still in the presence of him that dwelleth in light unapproachable.'

'Be still then, and know *that I. . .*' Who is your particular 'I'? Which bit of God most appeals to you? Who is your God-focus? Is it the Father, maker of heaven and earth and of all things visible and invisible, the transcendent God, wholly other, above and beyond us? Or is it the Son, is it the person of Christ, God revealed in a human life, the Jesus of the Gospels? Or is it the Holy Spirit, the breath, the energy of God, the life within all life, pulsating through life like a hidden dynamo? Which of these three aspects of God, so to speak, rings the loudest bell? Which is most real to you? That is your particular God-focus. Be content with that one aspect of God without worrying about the other two. Direct your prayer to that particular 'person' of God.

It may be that your God-focus will change over the months and the years. If it should, don't resist it – go along with it. If, for example, your God-focus is the person of Christ and then Christ begins to wane, to blackout on you, and instead there slowly comes into focus a sense of the Father, the transcendent God, or of the Holy Spirit, the breath and energy of God, don't try to hang on to Christ. Let him go and move on to the Father or the Holy Spirit. A. J. Balfour, who was both a philosopher and a politician, once wrote: 'Our highest truths are but half-truths. Think not to settle down for ever in any truth. Make use of it as a tent in which to pass a summer's night. But build no house of it, or it will be your tomb. When you first have an inkling of its insufficiency and begin to descry a dim counter-truth looming up beyond, then weep not, but give thanks. It is the Lord's voice whispering, "Take up thy bed and walk".'

'Be still then, and know that *I am God*.' God is the *living*

11

God, alive, personal, and present with you now. He is the great '*I am*'. And he is '*God*', the ultimate reality.

God has been experienced as Father, God transcendent, high and lifted up. He has been experienced as Son, God incarnate, God come down to earth and revealed in the human life of Jesus. He has been experienced as Holy Spirit, God immanent in creation, the Life within all life. And yet it is the same God who has been experienced. This is what the doctrine of the Trinity is trying to say. There are three Persons in one God. 'Three in one and one in three'. Now this is very difficult to understand. It sounds like nonsense until we realize that it is simply an attempt to put into human language, into a formula, how Christians have actually *experienced* God in their lives. All doctrines are like this. They are theological statements which attempt to formulate the experience of believers, to codify them, so that they become part of Christian tradition and can be passed on to subsequent generations.

God is *both* Father, Son and Holy Spirit, although *we* may be drawn to one particular 'person' or aspect of him rather than another. God is Alpha and Omega, the beginning and the end. He is the Ground of our being, 'the still point of the turning world'. He is the Absolute, the All. 'Be still then, and know that I am *God*.'

You may think that I have taken rather a long time over this. But it really is important. Don't think of it as a waste of your precious prayer time. It is essential to it. Tom Pym, who was a great teacher of prayer some years ago, wrote: 'We should remember that we cannot rush at prayer. If one has five minutes for prayer, two minutes of it should be used in preparation; if fifteen minutes are available for prayer, then the first four may be used in preparation.'

All right, having got myself reasonably relaxed and concentrated, where do I go from here? How shall I pray? What form should it take? That depends on you. Dom John Chapman wrote in his *Spiritual Letters*: 'Pray as you can, not as you can't.' You have got to find your own way, the way that 'clicks' with you. Otherwise, your prayer will be unreal, boring, a burden and you will eventually give it up; because you are trying to pray 'as you can't'. You are going against your natural grain. But you first need to know what the options are, what are the different ways of prayer.

There are three different ways of prayer. You can pray by using words, talking to God. This is called vocal prayer. Or you can pray by means of reading, thinking over what you have read and using your imagination. This is called mental prayer or meditation. Or you can pray in silence, just being still before God without words or thoughts or imagination. This is called silent prayer or contemplation.

Baron von Hügel, one of the giants among spiritual writers of this century, analysed religion into three elements which he called the institutional, the intellectual and the mystical. A fully-balanced religion, he said, will contain a bit of each element, but each individual will be drawn to one particular element rather than another. And that will dictate the way he or she will pray, whether through words or thoughts or silence. His advice was: follow your own particular inclination. Pray in the way which attracts you, appeals to you, the way which comes naturally.

If you are an institutional type, one who values tradition, appreciates being part of an institution, enjoys church services, likes to have things a bit cut and dried, then *perhaps* the best way of prayer for you is through words.

If you are an intellectual type, someone who likes reading and thinking over what you read, an imaginative person, then *perhaps* the best way of prayer for you is through thoughts.

If you are a mystical type, someone who can be alone, a seeker with a desire to know at first-hand, open to experience deep down, an intuitive rather than a rational person, then *perhaps* the best way of prayer for you is through silence.

But notice that I have emphasized 'perhaps'. Don't draw any conclusions yet. Let us have a look at each way of prayer in turn.

4

Through Words

Vocal prayer

You can use a book if you like, other people's words. Grand words which stimulate the spirit, or ordinary everyday words which you feel at home with. Using a book is like a musician using a score. It gives you something to follow. You don't have to improvise on your own. There are many such books of prayers. Shop around and find the right book for you.

But beware of formality, of what the Bible calls 'vain repetition', simply reading off the words full-stop. Take time over it.

The time may come when you get bored with a book. The words go dead on you, carry no meaning, give no stimulation. If and when this happens, that is a sign to change: from using other people's words to using your own, to stop following a music score and trying to improvise.

But you need to have some simple scheme in your mind to hold your attention and to keep a sense of proportion between the different parts of prayer. The best scheme I know is the word *ACTS*, each letter standing for a particular part of prayer.

A stands for *Adoration*. Be conscious of God's immensity and glory and try to express your wonder, admiration, worship and praise in words.

C stands for *Contrition*. Be conscious of yourself and the ways in which you have ignored or rejected God and 'crucified Christ afresh'; the ways in which you have hurt other people and failed to fulfil your potential. Confess the particular times and occasions which you remember. Express your sorrow for these sins and ask for the assurance of God's forgiveness.

But a warning here. If you are given to introspection, to

compulsive self-examination and a feeling of guilt, don't spend too long over *C*, or your prayer will become inward-looking and unhealthy. Move on quickly to *T*.

T stands for *Thanksgiving*. Be thankful to God who is the Giver of all good things and express your thankfulness in words. Take time over this and make it personal. Look around and select particular things for which you are genuinely grateful, like picking flowers in your garden, or turning over the pages of a photograph album. 'Count your blessings, count them one by one.' And say thank you to God for each one.

S stands for *Supplication*. The object of the exercise is not to inform God of what you want. He knows that already. Nor is it to wheedle things out of God for your own advantage. That would be a selfish using of God, a manipulation, an exploitation, which has no place in a love relationship. The object of the exercise is to put yourself, with all your desires, anxieties, problems, circumstances, duties, pleasures and pains, into the hands of God; and to be open to his influence, his inflowing life, so that his will may be done in you and through you. Supplication is not informing and wheedling. It is sharing and co-operating; talking to God about yourself and desiring to know and to do his will.

I am personally a bit shy about direct petition for particular things – give me this, take away that – because my desires are often so short-sighted and short-lived. What I want may be not what I need. And because the selfish using of God is so obvious a temptation. I prefer to concentrate on offering and sharing. I offer myself with all my needs and circumstances. I offer my work and my marriage. I offer up the coming day with all its commitments – where I shall go, what I shall do, whom I shall meet. I offer up any problems and anxieties which are on my mind, any decisions which I have to make. I share with God whatever is disturbing me. And behind it all is the desire 'thy will be done' in me and through me.

Under this heading of *Supplication*, you will not only remember yourself and your own needs. You will also remember other people and their needs. You are 'involved with mankind' and so you will remember the world and particular things which are happening in the world, things you have read about in the newspapers, heard on the radio, seen on television. You will also remember people whom you knew and loved on earth and who are now with God in eternal life.

Remembering other people before God is called intercession. What do you do? Just talk to God about these people and these things. Or hold them in your mind for a moment, have a picture of them and say their name.

It is a good thing to make a list of people and things you are going to pray for. The list will grow over the months and years and you will need to prune it a bit and to rearrange it, dividing it up between different days of the week. Otherwise it will become a burden, something to be got through. And that is no good, because it then becomes a mere formality, impersonal and unreal.

When you come to the end of the word *ACTS*, say the 'Our Father' very slowly. It is a wonderful prayer, covering everything. It is the Lord's Prayer. But when we say it in church, it is often said so quickly that it comes and goes before we know where we are. All the more reason then, when we are praying on our own, for saying it slowly, taking it clause by clause, thinking about it.

Through Thoughts

Meditation

This way of prayer is a mixture of reading, thinking, imagining and listening. It is more of a dialogue with God than a monologue. Opening our mind to God, brooding upon him. It is called mental prayer or meditation.

What exactly do you do?

First of all, you choose a passage to read. It should not be too long, because its purpose is simply to give your mind something to latch on to, to enable your mind and imagination to concentrate upon God.

Suppose you choose a passage from one of the four Gospels. You can choose a particular passage. Or you can work through a particular Gospel, beginning with Mark's which was the earliest Gospel to be written. Or you can take the *Bible Reading Fellowship Notes* which give you a particular passage for each day and supply you with notes on it.

Remember, when you are reading the Gospels, that they are faith documents. By that I mean that they were written from the other side of the resurrection. They were written by people who firmly believed in Jesus as the Son of God. They are not objective reports from 'our Middle East correspondent'. They are statements of faith to encourage believers and to challenge unbelievers. They originated from stories about Jesus which had been circulating among Christians for over thirty years. These stories and anecdotes were then collected and edited by the various Evangelists – Matthew, Mark, Luke and John. John's Gospel, by the way, which was the last to be written, reads more like a meditation upon the life and work of Jesus. There are long soliloquies, the Evangelist putting into the mouth of Jesus what he believed about him. Remember, also, that the Gospels come from a different age from ours, with different thought-forms, and coloured by the Jewish background of the early Christians. This will help you to understand them rather better and enable you to make allowances for what may well seem to be a strange way of thinking and imagining. They come from the first century, remember, and not the twentieth. The four Gospels are spiritual books communicating faith. They are very suitable for meditation, provided you bear these things in mind.

Having chosen your passage, ask the Holy Spirit to breathe upon the words you read and to make them come alive, to inspire your thoughts and to kindle your love. You can use that prayer to the Holy Spirit which we sometimes sing as a hymn. It was probably written in the ninth century.

> Come, Holy Ghost, our souls inspire,
> And lighten with celestial fire;
> Thou the anointing Spirit art,
> Who dost thy sevenfold gifts impart.
>
> Thy blessèd unction from above
> Is comfort, life and fire of love;
> Enable with perpetual light
> The dullness of our blinded sight.
>
> Anoint and cheer our soilèd face
> With the abundance of thy grace:
> Keep far our foes, give peace at home;
> Where thou art guide no ill can come.
>
> Teach us to know the Father, Son,
> And thee, of Both, to be but One;
> That through the ages all along
> This may be our endless song,
>
> 'Praise to thy eternal merit,
> Father, Son and Holy Spirit.'

Then read the passage slowly. If, in reading through the Gospels bit by bit, you come across a passage which you can't make head or tail of, don't panic. Skip it and move on to the next passage which does make sense.

Next, you *think* about the passage you have read, asking yourself three questions:

1 What does this mean? What is it all about? Use your imagination and build up the scene. Picture the characters in the story.

2 What does this mean *to me*? Is there anything God wants to say to me personally through this passage which I have read? What possible bearing has it on my life? Stop here and listen. Wait upon God for any illumination, insight, intuition to come. Or any stirring of your affections. Spend the main part of your prayer-time on this second question.

3 Is there anything I can do about it? Is there any practical thing I can do in response? Any resolution I can make?

There are thus three stages in a meditation. The first stage is that of consideration, looking at the passage you have read objectively. The second stage is that of communion, looking at the passage subjectively, as it applies to you. As an old man said to the Curé d'Ars: 'I look at him and he looks at me.' The third stage is that of co-operation, making some small practical resolution in response to what you have read and thought about.

Or, to put it more simply but dramatically:

Jesus before the eyes,
Jesus in the heart,
Jesus in the hands.

There are, of course, other ways of meditation. I have given you here what I think is the simplest and which has helped many people. It is called the Sulpician method and originated from the parish of St Sulpice in Paris in the seventeenth century.

This way of prayer will affect your intercession, the way you pray for other people and for the world. Instead of talking to God about people and situations in the world, you will *think* about them, imagine them, have a picture of them. And you will hold them up before God in your mind and imagination, so that they may catch something of his light and life and love and power.

As you grow in meditation, you will probably find that you will spend less time reading and thinking and more time just being still before God. A simple waiting upon him in faith and hope and love.

Or, you may find yourself spending time in what is called affective prayer. This is more a prayer of the heart than of the mind. You take some phrase which appeals to you, which kindles your affections and warms your heart. And you dwell on it, turning it over in your mind and tasting it, so to speak. You repeat it to yourself over and over again. You will find that it both lights up your mind and imagination, warms your affections and stirs your will. Years ago, Gilbert Shaw produced a whole book of affective phrases called *A Pilgrim's Book of Prayers*. But you could perfectly well do it yourself. You could, for example, break up the Lord's Prayer into its separate phrases and use them. Or the same thing with a favourite Psalm or hymn.

If you should feel moved to do this, you will find peace and joy and strength in this kind of prayer. It sometimes happens to people who are en route to silent or contemplative prayer. But we are all made differently and you must discover and follow your own way.

6

Through Silence

Contemplation

The time may come when you do not want to pray in words and you do not want to pray in thought. You just want to pray. To be still before God. To pray in silence. But how? What do you actually do in silent or contemplative prayer, as it is called?

The answer is: you do nothing! Now, that may sound a bit blunt and not very helpful. So let me try to explain.

You take some time over that relaxing exercise – 'Be still then,' – directing the stillness to your body and your nervous system, deliberately relaxing your muscles. Then you direct the stillness to your whirling mind, emptying it of all thought and imagination, so far as you can, closing your eyes. And finally you direct the stillness to your spirit, to you deep down, plunging yourself and losing yourself in the stillness.

When you have got yourself still and relaxed, move on to the rest of that verse from the Psalm – 'and know' – know deep down, know without thought, without feeling, just know 'that I am God'.

When you reach the word 'God', believe that your will is fixed upon God. That, at a deep level, below thought and imagination and feeling, you are open to God and God is open to you. That you are in communication.

But because this communication is at a deep level, below surface thoughts, imaginings and emotions, it is experienced as darkness.

I said to my soul, be still, and let the dark come upon you
Which shall be the darkness of God . . .

21

But the faith and the love and the hope are all in the
  waiting . . .
So the darkness shall be the light, and the stillness the
  dancing.

T. S. Eliot, 'East Coker'

Enter into this darkness wherein is the mystery of God. And
then just stay there for as long a time as you have set yourself
to pray. Don't try to do anything, to say anything, to think
anything. Just stay where you are, 'sitting and doing nothing
in front of God', as Archbishop Anthony Bloom has put it.
That is your prayer – to stay there in the silence and the
darkness, your will fixed upon God deep down, until the clock
strikes. Whatever it feels like, your prayer is going on, you are
in communication with God, for as long as you remain where
you are. It only stops when you get up from your chair and
walk out of the room.

It is very important to remember this, to believe this, because
all sorts of strange things may happen during this time of silent
prayer!

First of all, your mind and imagination will wander all over
the place, like a bee seeking honey. And your will won't be
able to control them. Because your will is otherwise engaged.
It is fixed upon God deep down. And your will can't do two
things at once. So your mind and imagination are free to
wander.

Try not to worry about this. It is irritating and disturbing,
like flies on a hot day when you are having a picnic. But
that doesn't stop you having a picnic. Nor should wandering
thoughts and imaginings stop your silent prayer. Apply to yourself some words Baron von Hügel wrote about irritation: 'Bear
it gently, like a fever or a toothache . . . just ignore all that
rumpus.' As a Zen master put it in a typically Buddhist way:
'Do not try to think; and do not try not to think.' Relax. Let
the thoughts come and go, but you just stay where you are,
centred on God.

Of course, you should not deliberately follow up any
wandering thought which comes along. Because that would be

to take your will away from what it should be doing, which is to remain fixed upon God. And when you find that you *have* followed one up without realizing it, drop it at once like a red-hot coal and fix your will again steadily upon God.

You can, if you like, introduce into your prayer words of one syllable, like 'God' or 'love'. They should only be of one syllable, otherwise you will start thinking about them. This is the advice of the anonymous author of *The Cloud of Unknowing*, a classic book on silent or contemplative prayer written towards the end of the fourteenth century. These one-syllable words are not your prayer, but they can be useful weapons. 'With this word you will hammer the cloud and the darkness above you. With this word you will suppress all thought under the cloud of forgetting.'*

Another strange thing which may happen in silent prayer is the bubbling-up of our unconscious memory. In this kind of prayer, our whole self is exposed to the light and love and power of God, including our unconscious memory where all our buried fears and phantoms lie. Bringing these unconscious memories up to the surface can be disturbing. As Fr Michael Hollings has said: 'In silent prayer, the scum of one's life can arise, the reality of me, things I hadn't realized about myself.' Nevertheless, however painful, this is a healing process. It exposes our 'shadow side' to the light and the love and the power of God, enabling us to accept it and to live with it, making us whole.

Another thing which can happen in silent prayer is despair. We feel that we are doing nothing, that nothing is happening; that this is not prayer at all but a complete waste of time. And yet, if someone walked into the room while we were engaged in this strange activity, we should know that we were being interrupted. Interrupted in what? Something must have been going on after all!

The author of *The Cloud of Unknowing* wrote another treatise, called *The Epistle of Privy Counsel*. It was probably written for

---

* *The Cloud of Unknowing* is available in the Penguin Classics.

the same person as *The Cloud*, at a later stage of his or her spiritual journey. He describes silent or contemplative prayer as 'the bare reaching of your will towards God . . . the simple reaching out to God'. Meister Eckhart, in his sermons and treatises delivered in the same fourteenth century, says the same thing. We are to remain in the silence and the darkness, 'facing straight, with no side glances towards the Eternal Word'.

God is not like anything. He cannot be compared with anything, thought about or imagined. Therefore, in order to know God, we have to enter into darkness. In order to receive God, we have to become nothing – bare, empty, desolate. But, as Eckhart says, this bare, empty, desolate nothingness is the place of 'potential receptivity'. It is the place where we 'gain Him who is all things . . . God pours himself into you', and we receive him 'unawares'.

Sometimes we are aware of God deep down and sometimes we are not. But, whether we are aware of him or not, we are open to God and we are receiving God all the time. We receive him without realizing it. We receive him 'unawares'. And as a result, we find that outside our time of prayer we are able to see God in all things. 'All things', says Eckhart, 'become simply God to you, for in all things you notice only God, just as a man who stares at the sun sees the sun in whatever he afterwards looks at.'

This is one of the effects of silent or contemplative prayer. Other effects are certain character changes. We gradually become a little bit more humble, a little bit more sensitive, a little bit more free, a little bit more peaceful, a little bit more trusting, a little bit more just wanting to do God's will. 'By their fruits you shall know them.'

Both the author of *The Cloud of Unknowing* and Meister Eckhart say that those who pray silently should intercede silently. They should direct their prayer to God for people and for the world in general and not in particular. I have no need to mention particular people or particular situations in my prayer, because God already knows who and what is on my mind. It is enough for me simply to offer to him a part of my silent prayer in intercession for all men, horizontally embracing the earth. This can be a great liberation. I have personally found, strangely enough, that I give more time to intercession this way, than I ever did when I prayed for people by name or in thought.

A friend of mine, Canon John Townroe, wrote an article on silent or contemplative prayer, which he deliberately called 'Prayer for Busy People'. That is worth thinking about. I have found in experience that this is the best way of prayer for many people today, although they do not realize it until they try. But when they do, they find it to be a real way-in to God.

But it is not everyone's way. We must each find our own way. We must each pray as we can and not as we can't. Moreover, our spiritual life needs to be balanced, inclusive not exclusive, flexible not rigid. Let that wise man, Baron von Hügel, have the last word. 'Let me then suggest that we should each of us discover what is the form of prayer to which God appears to call us; let us give ample room and opportunity to this particular form; but let us also organize a certain regular amount of the other kinds of prayer and worship.' Thus shall we have a truly balanced spiritual life, 'safe and wholesome'.

7

Through 'Quickies'

On waking up, going to sleep and all through the day

The title of this chapter does not refer to fast bowlers! Nor does it refer to one of the elements in a radio or television quiz programme. It refers to what are called ejaculatory prayers or arrow prayers – quick darts of prayer which we shoot up to God, first thing in the morning, last thing at night and at odd times during the day.

For example:

When we wake up in the morning, a quick 'This is the day the Lord has made; we will be glad and rejoice in it. Alleluia!'

When we turn out the light at night and settle down to sleep, a quick 'Father, into thy hands I commend my spirit'; or 'I will lay me down in peace and take my rest, for it is thou, Lord, only that makest me dwell in safety'; or 'Save us, O Lord, while waking and guard us while sleeping, that awake we may watch with Christ and asleep we may rest in peace'. (I have used traditional language here, but you can happily abbreviate it and modernize it to suit your own taste.)

And at odd moments during the day. For example:

In moments of thankfulness and joy, a quick 'Thanks be to God.'

In moments of anxiety, a quick 'Father, into thy hands.'

In moments of fear, a quick 'Lord, hold me', 'Lord save me.'

In moments of doubt and indecision, a quick 'Lord, guide me.'

In moments of weakness and temptation, a quick 'Lord, strengthen me.'

In moments of sin, a quick 'Lord, have mercy.'

(Again, use any words which come naturally and fit your particular mood and need.)

And before anything we do – especially if we are a bit scared about saying and doing the right thing. For example, before answering the telephone, writing a letter, going up to talk to someone, before going in to an interview, etc. – a quick 'Lord, use me'. And after we have done it, however it appears to have gone, a quick 'Thank you, Lord, for using me'.

But suppose it went badly? Suppose we made a complete mess of things? How could God have used us? Surely, he obviously didn't. So wouldn't it be nonsense to say 'Thank you, Lord, for using me'? However, wait a minute. Let me tell you a story – a true story.

A priest called Dr Reginald Somerset-Ward was one of the great spiritual directors or counsellors in the Anglican Church of this century. One of the first people who came to see him was a woman who was in great difficulty. He listened to her, talked to her and afterwards wrote her a letter. Before writing the letter, he had said 'Lord, use me' and as he dropped the envelope into the letter-box, he said 'Thank you, Lord, for using me'. Now, as a result of this letter, the woman lost her faith altogether! How, then, could God have used the writer of that letter? But – and this is the point – two years later, the same woman wrote to Dr Somerset-Ward to say that as a consequence of that letter, which she had pondered over all this time, she had come to a stronger faith and a deeper desire for God, and please could she come to see him again! So, God *did* use that letter-writer after all, in spite of the evidence to the contrary. This is worth remembering.

To say 'Lord, use me' before anything we do, especially if we are a bit scared, is a sheer act of faith. We are never really the judge of our own performance. So we can, by an equal act of faith, say 'Thank you, Lord, for using me,' however it *seems* to have gone. Because you never know what may happen.

Prayer is not confined to our set times of prayer. It should flow over and fill the whole day. So it is a good thing deliberately to make short arrow prayers – a word, a phrase – all through the day. It brings God into the ordinary, everyday events of living and keeps us mindful of his presence with us wherever we are and whatever we are doing.

Choose a word or a phrase which appeals to you and have it on the tip of your tongue. Train yourself deliberately to use this word or phrase – for example, when you walk in and out of a room, when you go upstairs, when you make the beds, when you wash up, when you sit down, when you go out into the garden. Until, bit by bit, it becomes a habit.

Eastern Orthodox Christians have a phrase which they have used from the very early centuries. It is called The Jesus Prayer, and consists in saying the words 'Lord Jesus Christ, Son of God, have mercy on me a sinner'. They use it in their set times of prayer as a sort of background to silent prayer. But it can be used at any time and anywhere – waiting at a bus stop, on the Tube, while shaving, brushing your teeth, going for a walk, etc.

Beside these vocal arrow prayers which we say, as it were, under our breath, there are also visual 'quickies' to meet our particular needs. A word or a phrase which we write down and keep in our handbag or wallet, on the desk or the dressing table – somewhere where we come across it. For example, if we have a fear about our own value: 'I am loved by God.' If we have a fear about our own ability: 'I am upheld by God, used by God' or 'God is doing the work'. If we have a tendency to moods of anxiety, insecurity and depression which descend on us like a great black cloud, blotting out everything except a sense of our own misery and hopelessness: 'This will lift.'

Or, if you want something a bit longer, there is St Teresa's Bookmark:

> Let nothing disturb thee
> Nothing affright thee;
> All things are passing,
> God never changeth;
> Patient endurance
> Attaineth to all things;

Who God possesseth
In nothing is wanting;
Alone God sufficeth.

Christian ejaculatory prayer is very like the Hindu or Buddhist mantra – a prayerful sound or thought contained in a word or phrase. Christoper Isherwood has something very interesting to say about the mantra and its effects on our life in his book *Ramakrishna and his Disciples*.

> We are creatures of reverie, not of reason. We spend a very small proportion of our time thinking logical, consecutive thoughts. It is within the reverie that our passions and prejudices – often so terrible in their consequences – build themselves up, almost unnoticed, out of slogans, newspaper headlines, chance-heard words of fear and greed and hate, which have slipped into our consciousness through our unguarded eyes and ears. Our reverie expresses what we are, at any given moment. The mantra, by introducing God into the reverie, must produce profound subliminal changes. These may not be apparent for some time, but sooner or later, they will inevitably appear – first in the prevailing mood and disposition of the individual; then in a gradual change of character.

What do you think about when you are sitting doing nothing? Yourself? Your grievances? The difficult neighbours? The state of the country, the state of the world? Or just nothing in particular? Then introduce God into your sitting and doing nothing, into your reverie. Or into those automatic activities which don't need much concentration. Introduce God into the waste places of your day. This, in time, will bear positive fruit in your life.

Whether we pray best in words or through thoughts or in silence, ejaculatory prayer is something which we can *all* do. And then we shall be praying, as St Paul advised, all day long. 'Pray constantly', he wrote in one of his letters. A great Russian scholar of the Orthodox Church wrote: 'The true aim of prayer is to enter into conversation with God. It is not restricted to certain hours of the day. A Christian has to feel himself personally in the presence of God. The goal of prayer is precisely to be with God always.'

8

The Difficulty of Concentration

Wandering thoughts

To repeat what I said earlier. Prayer is a very strange activity. It is an attempt to communicate with a Being who is inaccessible to our ordinary senses, inaccessible to reason, inaccessible to science. To believe in God and to pray is a sheer act, a wager, a leap, of faith.

So we should expect prayer to be difficult; just because it is so very different from all our other activities.

It is a good thing, if you can find the right person, to have a 'soul-friend', a spiritual director or counsellor, who can befriend and guide you and help you to find your way through all the difficulties and experiences which you may encounter. It is hard to go-it-alone in the spiritual life. We all need help, guidance, and above all, encouragement. Kenneth Leech writes in *True God*: '. . . the soul-friend, the spiritual companion or guide, is of crucial importance, for we all need to be held, warmly, firmly, and with the reassurance that we are still whole, still travelling, still safe.' It is a good thing to be able to talk to someone from time to time – not only about prayer, but about anything and everything – someone to share things with.

A priest ought to be a good soul-friend. But it need not be a priest. It could be any wise and experienced person, male or female. But as with choosing the right spiritual book to read, it must be a person with whom you 'click', a person you feel at home with and with whom you can be yourself. I hope that you may be able to discover such a person.

But meanwhile, in the next four chapters, I shall do my best to help with the various difficulties and experiences which we meet along the way in this strange activity.

First of all, there is the difficulty of concentration.

We settle ourselves down to pray and our thoughts go wandering off all over the place. And often they are such trivial thoughts! What shall we have for supper? I wonder how Bob's getting on? Oh dear, I don't think I've got any onions and it's half-day closing. Did I say I'd be home late, I can't remember? Well, maybe I won't, if only Jim gets a move on. He's so slow. Spends half his time talking to Betty. I wonder what they talk about? Do you think he's keen on her? Jean doesn't like her. Football for the boys this afternoon. Hope Mike does well. Oh dear, it's raining. And I did want to cut the grass. I do wish next door wouldn't have the radio on so loud; or is it the television? (And so on and so on.)

But please don't get too depressed about it. And don't despair. It's natural that your mind should wander. It hasn't got anything tangible to hang on to, to hold its attention. Your mind is used to concentrating on tangible things and God is intangible. Spiritual concentration is a new thing. It takes time and practice to learn. But it will gradually come if you persevere.

When you are aware that your mind has wandered off, just gently bring it back to where you were and try to concentrate again upon God. Your prayer time may well be spent like this – your mind wandering off and being pulled back. That is how you learn, how you train your mind to concentrate upon God. By endlessly pulling it back to him.

Sometimes, of course, your wandering thoughts aren't so much trivial, as anxious. You've got something on your mind and it keeps coming into your mind whenever you try to pray. It may be a difficult letter you have to write or a problem you have to work out or a tricky situation you have to face, or something you have to remember.

Perhaps the best thing to do here is to offer the anxiety to God: 'Father, into thy hands'. And to try to leave it there with him. But back it will come. And back to God it must go, over and over again.

On the other hand, some people find when they are plagued

with an anxious thought which nags at them, that it is better to write it down; for example, 'I *must* ring the children's head-master before he leaves'. Then they find they can 'flop' it. I'm not so sure about this myself. It seems to me that you could spend the whole of your prayer time writing little memos! I personally prefer the way of offering, but I thought that perhaps I should mention this other way.

When you are ill or overstrained, and as you grow old, your ability to concentrate will vary alarmingly from day to day. Then you have to be very humble and accept the situation. Accept your limitations and just do the best you can without expecting too much. And please don't get cross with yourself. That is no use to anyone, least of all to God.

Wandering thoughts are very common. Everyone suffers from them, even the most spiritual people. John Donne the poet, who became Dean of St Paul's, wrote: 'Even the rustling of a straw makes me look up from my prayers.' That should be a comfort to you and an encouragement!

Wandering thoughts are not sinful if they are involuntary. They only become sinful if we deliberately choose to switch our attention off God and to give it instead to the wandering thought. But even then, we can pull ourselves up and pull ourselves back by a quick 'Lord, have mercy'. God understands our weakness and God forgives.

Our concentration in prayer is greatly helped by choosing the right time for us to pray and the right place. A time when we are reasonably relaxed and not overtired. A place where we are not going to be disturbed and which has the right kind of atmosphere. It is also greatly helped by spending the first few minutes deliberately trying to get still and relaxed, to settle down and to centre down. 'Be still then, and know that I am God.' Take each phrase in turn and dwell on it. This prepara-tory exercise really does pay dividends as regards our ability to concentrate in prayer.

9

The Difficulty about Feelings

Two difficulties

The first difficulty is this: sometimes we feel like praying and sometimes we don't. There is the temptation only to pray when we feel like it. And even to feel that it is hypocritical to pray when we don't.

Oh dear! All this emphasis upon our feelings! The fact is that our feelings are superficial and variable. They are dependent upon such things as the state of the weather, the state of our digestion, the time of the month, our moods, our circumstances. In everyday life we have to disregard our feelings, or we should never get up on a Monday morning and get the children off to school and get to work on time. And so on. Surely the same thing applies to prayer. If we only pray when we feel like it, we are making the activity of prayer – and even the reality of God – dependent upon our subjective feelings which vary from day to day. We are making the state of me, and how I feel, bigger than God. This is where having a Rule of Prayer helps. It ties us down. It keeps us at it, even on our worst day.

In everyday life we don't feel hypocritical when we try very hard to be patient with someone who drives us up the wall, instead of biting that person's head off, which is what we feel like doing. In fact, we are rather pleased with ourselves when we manage to do this. We have won the battle of will over feelings, achieved a victory of the deep part of us over our superficial, shallow selves. This is what we should try to do in prayer. Our will should conquer our feelings.

In this battle of will over feelings, the supreme example is Jesus on the cross. His feelings must have been outraged by the treatment which he received from his fellow men, the physical and mental cruelty. And also by the treatment which he seemed to receive from God his Father – the sense of darkness and forsakenness which came over him. And yet, and yet, in spite of all those outraged feelings, his will still held. He died in faith, as he had lived in faith. 'Father, into thy hands I commend my spirit.'

The second difficulty connected with feelings is this: sometimes we are conscious of the presence of God in our prayer and sometimes we are not. Sometimes we feel love and devotion and sometimes we don't. Sometimes our prayer is full of light and warmth and sometimes it is dark and cold.

There is a great danger of measuring the worth, the value of our prayer by the feelings which we have or don't have. When we are conscious of God and feel love and devotion, we say that our prayer has been real and worthwhile. But when we have been unconscious of any presence, unconscious of any love, then we say that our prayer has been unreal and a waste of time.

Now this is a temptation which we must learn to resist. It is not true that the value of your prayer depends upon the feelings which you have or don't have. That is to be subjective again. Prayer is an expression of faith, not of feeling. Our part in prayer is simply to give the time and to make the effort. We have no control over the feelings which we receive or don't receive. Our prayer has been real and worthwhile if we have kept the time we set ourselves and made the effort to attend to God. Any feelings we receive are a bonus.

Of course, it feels much better when we have been full of light and warmth. But don't be fooled by that. Our feelings are not the yardstick. They come and they go. If you only pray when it feels good, you are putting you and your feelings above your faith and your will. Measure the worth, the value of your prayer, not by the feelings which you receive or don't receive, but by the time you give, the effort you make and by the effects which your prayer gradually has upon your life and character and relationships.

There is a great emphasis today on spiritual *experience*. I am personally sympathetic to this. For me, the best argument for belief in God is the argument from religious experience. But spiritual experience is two-sided – outward and inward. From St Paul onwards, all the great teachers of spirituality have soft-pedalled the outward and emphasized the inward. And they have never equated the two.

Visions, locutions (seeing, hearing), sense-impressions (feeling, tasting, smelling), speaking in tongues – all these are outward manifestations of spiritual experience. They are gifts of God, to be received gratefully and joyfully, if and when they come. But they should not be sought after, clutched at, overvalued. Neither should we be puffed up by them. Nor should they be regarded as an infallible test and proof of the Spirit.

A friend of mine, on a lecture tour in the United States, was taken to a Pentecostal church run by a rather powerful lady. She asked him: 'Have you received the Spirit?' He replied Yes, he thought that he had. 'Do you speak in tongues?' she asked. And when he replied No, she said: 'Then you haven't received the Spirit.' And that was that! Q.e.d.

The reality of our spiritual life doesn't lie here, in these outward, physical manifestations. These are but the bubblings-up and the boiling-over of the Spirit. The reality of our spiritual life is an inward experience, gradually producing a change of character, a different attitude towards our fellow human beings and indeed towards the whole of God's creation. At Pentecost, the important thing is not the wind and the fire, but the inward power which people experienced, transforming their lives. In his first letter to the Christians in Corinth, St Paul wrote that the important thing is not speaking in tongues, but self-forgetting, self-giving love. 'By their fruits you shall know them.' That was Christ's yardstick for measuring spiritual reality.

Visions, locutions, sense-impressions, speaking in tongues – all these may be gifts of the spirit, but they are not the fruits of the spirit. St Paul wrote to the Christians in Galatia that the fruits of the spirit are 'love, joy, peace, patience, kindness, goodness, faithfulness, gentleness, self-control'.

When warm feelings and outward forms of spiritual experience come – if they should – we should enjoy them, thank God for them, use them. But we should not get our sums wrong. We should not be seduced by them into pride and superiority. Neither should we try to hang on to them. We should let them come and let them go. We should not put our trust in them. We should put our trust in God.

10

The Experience of Dryness

Spiritual fed-upness

There are periods in our lives when all that we experience in prayer is a sense of utter darkness and dryness. There is no light at all. God is blacked out. And we feel forsaken and rejected. That is what Jesus must have felt upon the cross shortly before he died. 'And at the ninth hour Jesus cried with a loud voice, "My God, my God, why hast thou forsaken me?" ' So we are sharing in his experience. You would have thought that would give us comfort and even a sense of union with Christ. But it doesn't. Because sometimes we are faced not only with darkness without, but also with a sense of dryness within. Our feelings are all dried up. We can't feel a thing, except possibly a sense of boredom, a spiritual fed-upness.

Now that, perhaps, is an extreme case – when darkness and dryness come together; when we are not only shut up in a spiritual Alcatraz (a prison off the coast of San Francisco where prisoners were locked up in a blacked-out cell called the black hole), but when we have no feeling either, no desire for God at all.

Very often, these two experiences are separate. Our feelings are dried up, but we are not submerged in utter darkness. And on the other hand, we are plunged into utter darkness, but we still have a desire for God.

Let me then separate these two things – although they *may* come together.

First, in this chapter, the sense of dryness.

Remember those words I quoted of Father Andrew: 'Prayer is you praying.' The state of *you*, physical, mental, nervous, circumstantial, will affect your prayer; because we are made all of a piece and that which affects one part of us will affect the rest.

Therefore, ask yourself: Am I overtired? Overstrained? Am I getting flu? Getting over an operation? Have I got too much on my plate? Am I in a state of anxiety? All these things will affect your prayer, drying up your desire. Prayer will be too much of an effort and your feelings will go on strike.

In which case, the way to tackle the problem, get over the difficulty, is to slow down, to calm down, to get better, to take things a bit easier, to give yourself more time, to get rid of some of your commitments, until your desire wakes up again. And meanwhile, just do the best you can as regards your prayer.

Also ask yourself: Does this dried-up feeling, this tiredness, boredom, fed-upness, apply to other activities in my life? What about my reading? Can I read easily, peacefully, enjoyably, a fairly serious book? Or is it too much of an effort? Am I able to concentrate? Or do I quickly get bored and prefer to watch the television.

If so, this is a sign which confirms that you are overtired or overstrained or overanxious or that your life is overfull. And so you need, first of all, to alter your life-style, or wait for circumstances to change, as the case may be, before the state of dryness in your prayer can lift.

On the other hand, you may answer these questions quite differently. You may not be able to see any physical, mental, nervous or circumstantial reason to account for your dried-upness in prayer. You are full of life and interest in all your other activities, able to concentrate on what you are doing, able to enjoy things. In that case, there must be a spiritual reason for your dryness.

Maybe you have got into a groove in your prayer. You are stuck in it. You are bored with it. It has gone dead on you. It has become a meaningless routine. In which case, this experience is a call to change your way of prayer. From saying words to reading and thinking, from reading and thinking to taking one phrase and savouring it, or to just being silent before God without words or thoughts or affections. Or vice versa: from silence to thoughts, from thoughts to words. Experiment and see which works.

This happened to me recently. For years, my way of prayer was silent prayer or contemplation. Then came a period of extreme dryness and I picked up a book of affective phrases – Gilbert Shaw's *A Pilgrim's Book of Prayers* – which I hadn't used for forty years! And it did the trick. My prayer became alive again. I don't use it all the time, but I know that it is there when I need it. Sometimes a change of image, the use of a different kind of language, different words, can stir the imagination and rekindle desire.

On the other hand, this experience may be a call to deepen your prayer; to root it in your bare will and not in your feelings. Thus your desire is taken away. And you have to learn to build your prayer upon rock and not upon sand.

Or, this experience may be a test of your love. A call to love God for himself alone and not for any feelings which he gives you. To love him 'for love's sake only'. In the first chapter of this book I quoted two lines of a poem by Elizabeth Barrett to Robert Browning. Let me complete that sonnet:

If thou must love me, let it be for naught
Except for love's sake only. Do not say
'I love her for her smile . . . her look . . . her way
Of speaking gently, . . . for a trick of thought
That falls in well with mine, and certes brought
A sense of pleasant ease on such a day' –
For these things in themselves, Belovèd, may
Be changed, or change for thee, – and love, so wrought,
May be unwrought so. Neither love me for
Thine own dear pity's wiping my cheeks dry, –
A creature might forget to weep, who bore
Thy comfort long, and lose thy love thereby!
But love me for love's sake, that evermore
Thou may'st love on, through love's eternity.

I know that it is very hard to pray when we are entirely unfeeling and lacking in desire. But, if we *can* manage to do this, then we really *are* loving God 'for love's sake only'. We are *giving* to God and not seeking for any reward except that of knowing that we do his will. And that is a pure act of love.

11

The Experience of Darkness

Spiritual blackout

Now for the experience of darkness. What about that?

First of all, ask yourself the same questions which you asked about the sense of dryness. Is there a physical cause? Or a mental or nervous cause? Or a circumstantial cause? If so, then follow the same treatment which I advised in the case of dryness.

Ask yourself also whether there is possibly a moral cause. Whether there is some unconfessed sin sitting on your conscience, filling you with a sense of guilt; and which operates like a dark cloud, separating you from God and shutting out the light of the sun. If so, you must repent of whatever it is, confess your sin and seek the forgiveness of God. Perhaps through the sacrament of penance and absolution, in which the priest, with the authority of Christ, brings to you the assurance of God's total and absolute forgiveness, restoring you to intimacy.

But if you cannot detect any physical, mental, nervous, circumstantial or moral cause for your sense of utter darkness, then there must be a spiritual cause. It must be God himself who is switching off the light and turning off the heat. But why on earth should God do that?

Since God is Love and since he loves you personally, it must be 'for love's sake only'. But how?

As in the case of dryness, it may be to test your love. Or to deepen your prayer. Or, not only to change your way of prayer, but to shift the whole of your God-focus.

May I share with you my own experience here? My God-focus was the discovery of Christ as the revelation of God in a human life. The other two Persons of the Trinity, the Father and the Holy Spirit, did not mean anything to me heartwise, although I understood their theological importance with my mind. The Person of Christ was my God-focus and my prayer in consequence was through meditation – reading a bit of the Gospels and thinking about it, dwelling on it, seeing where it applied to my own life. Well, one day and quite out of the blue, it seemed, the Person of Christ blacked out on me. And since he was the only God-Person I had, I was totally and absolutely in the dark. I did all the wrong things. I blamed myself. It was my sins which had come between me and God, although I wasn't aware of any particular sin which could do this awful thing to me. I must have lost my faith, although I couldn't think exactly why or when or where. I hadn't been trying hard enough in my prayer, so I tried harder, I prayed longer. But the harder I tried and the longer I prayed, the worse the darkness became. Finally, I gave up in despair.

Then one day I went to see a friend in St Albans. While staying with him, I strolled idly into the Abbey and just sat there in the nave looking at the east window in a vague sort of way. And gradually, for no reason at all, there came into my consciousness something I had never experienced before: a sense of the transcendence of God, the holiness of God, the awe-full-ness of God. The sense of God came back. But it was not focused on the Person of Christ. The Person of Christ had died on me, except intellectually. Spiritually, it was now the sense of God the Father, of the immense, absolute, awe-inspiring transcendence of God. And I knelt down before this new vision of God and worshipped. And my prayer changed from reading and thinking to silence, from meditation to contemplation.

I have told this story perhaps overdramatically. Perhaps it did not happen quite as suddenly as that. But it certainly happened. And it changed my spiritual life. I can see now that my experience of darkness was given to me by God 'for love's sake only', forcing me to shift my God-focus from the Person of Christ to the Person of the Father. And to change my way of prayer in consequence.

> Who then devised the torment? Love.
> Love is the unfamiliar name
> Behind the hands that wove
> The intolerable shirt of flame
> Which human power cannot remove.
>
> T. S. Eliot, 'Little Gidding'

I should like to say this to people who are suffering from darkness or dryness in their prayer – or from both: try not to fuss. Don't blame yourself. Don't force yourself spiritually. Try, if you possibly can, to keep the time you have set yourself to pray, even if all that you can do in that time is to say words or to read a book. Above all, try to trust – even though it will be a blind trust. Trust and wait. Wait for something to happen. God may be testing your love, deepening your prayer, changing your way of prayer, changing your whole God-focus. Wait and see in blind trust.

> I said to my soul, be still, and wait without hope
> For hope would be hope for the wrong thing; wait without love
> For love would be love of the wrong thing; there is yet faith
> But the faith and the love and the hope are all in the waiting.
> Wait without thought, for you are not ready for thought:
> So the darkness shall be the light, and the stillness the dancing.
>
> T. S. Eliot, 'East Coker'

Mind you, for some people – those whose way of prayer is silent or contemplative – this experience of darkness is a very positive experience, a way of meeting God.

In the Book of Exodus and in the Psalms, there are several references to God dwelling in darkness and cloud. 'And the Lord said to Moses, "Lo, I am coming to you in a thick cloud. . ." And the people stood afar off, while Moses drew near to the thick cloud where God was. . . Then Moses went up on the mountain, and the cloud covered the mountain. The glory of the Lord settled on Mount Sinai and the cloud covered it six days and on the seventh day he called to Moses out of the midst of the cloud. . .' 'He made darkness his secret place; his pavilion round about him with dark water, and thick clouds to cover him. . .' 'Clouds and darkness are round about him.'

No wonder that fourteenth-century anonymous author chose as the title for his book on contemplation *The Cloud of Unknowing*. No wonder, two centuries later, that St John of the Cross called his two great books for those beginning and those practising contemplative prayer *The Ascent of Mount Carmel* and *The Dark Night of the Soul*.

In silent or contemplative prayer, we have to live with darkness. We have willingly to enter into that dark cloud where God dwells, beyond the reach of words or thoughts.

To begin with, it is comparatively easy. Because, to begin with, it is not all dark. It is a new experience and there are flashes of light and some excitement. But that is just to get us going, to encourage us to abandon ourselves in trust and to enter into the darkness where God dwells in mystery. But the light soon fades and the excitement passes. And we are left in the darkness with only our bare will, the will of faith, to keep us there. Yet, in this darkness, we are aware – at least sometimes – of a mysterious presence, a reality. And we are aware that in this way of prayer, it is God who is holding us rather than we who are holding God.

Nevertheless, we do go through black periods in contemplative prayer, when this abandonment in faith is very difficult and at times almost impossible to bear. When this happens, you may find that you have to inject into your silent prayer some affective phrases – not just one-syllable words. Or to spend some of the time just reading a spiritual book – perhaps an old book which you haven't looked at for years.

Yet, if you can manage to persevere in silent prayer, you will discover, slowly but surely, a sense of deep peace underneath all the stress, a deep security underneath all the insecurity and almost a deep sense of joy underneath all the gloom. As Augustine Baker wrote in the seventeenth century, in his book *Holy Wisdom*: 'Out of this darkness God produces light and strength . . . tranquillity of mind in the midst of a tempest of passions . . . patience in the midst of impatience . . . resignation in the midst of irresignation.' A triumph of grace indeed!

12

The Need for Perseverance

The keyword in prayer

We have come to the end of this book. I want to leave you
with one word before I say Good-bye, which means 'God be
with you'. That one word, the keyword in prayer, is
perseverance.

'It is perseverance in the spiritual life, on and on, across the
years and the changes of our moods and trials, health and
environment; it is this that supremely matters.' So wrote Baron
von Hügel, perhaps unconsciously echoing the words of Jesus:
'No man, having put his hand to the plough and looking back,
is fit for the Kingdom of God.'

Jesus, of course, was the supreme example of this virtue of
perseverance. There must have been times when he was
tempted to despair. But, so far as we know, he never gave way
to despair. He persevered. He went on. On his way up to
Jerusalem, he met with an early rebuff. A Samaritan village
rejected him. Yet he went on – by way of another village.
And when he arrived in Jerusalem, he met with more rebuffs:
misunderstanding, opposition, hostility, rejection, arrest,
betrayal, desertion, false accusation, condemnation, ridicule,
torture, crucifixion. Yet he went on through it all. He went on
teaching, healing, loving. By keeping his hand on the plough,
by going on, by his perseverance, Jesus proved himself to be
a King. 'Behold your King!' Pilate spoke truer than he knew.

Jesus taught people. He lavished time and care especially on
a small group of disciples, patiently teaching them new truths
or old truths in a new light. Yet, in spite of it all, they remained
thick, closed-minded, limited, set in their old ways. There are

few more tragic moments in the gospel story than the moment when Jesus overheard the disciples quarrelling in the upper room in Jerusalem before the Last Supper, quarrelling about which of them was the greatest, competing for status. Was not this a moment for despair? What's the use? Why go on? Yet Jesus went on. He took a towel and a bowl of water and went round to the disciples in turn and washed their feet, driving home through an acted parable the lesson of the royalty of service.

Jesus healed people. Quite a part of his ministry was devoted to healing the sick in body and mind. Yet his works of healing were misunderstood and even taken down and used in evidence against him. 'He casts out demons by Beelzebub, the prince of demons.' He is in league with the devil! Yet Jesus went on. He healed the sick in Jerusalem as in Galilee. He was not put off by misunderstanding and misrepresentation. He perserved in his work.

Jesus loved people. He really cared for people as people. He mixed with and made friends with all sorts and conditions. He did not distinguish between the religious and the irreligious, the righteous and unrighteous in his relationships. But this was misunderstood and misinterpreted. He is not a good man, a holy man, or he would have nothing to do with these disreputable and irreligious people. He is a worldly man, a sensual man. Birds of a feather flock together! He is a 'gluttonous man and a wine-bibber, the friend of tax-collectors and sinners'. Yet Jesus went on, risking his reputation, persevering in his love of people, irrespective of their appearance.

But it was in Jerusalem that his faith and his love were most severely tested. Could they stand up in the face of rejection by authority, betrayal by a close friend, the sneers and the ridicule, being pilloried as a criminal and, finally, the excruciating agony of crucifixion? And the sense of forsakenness as he hung dying on the cross? Yet Jesus went on. His faith and his love still held. He persevered to the very end. 'Then said Jesus', as he hung suspended on the cross, 'Father, forgive them, for they know not what they do. . .' 'It is finished . . . Father, into thy hands I commend my spirit.' Thus he died, undiminished and undefeated.

In this strange activity of prayer, we are on a journey which passes through changing scenery, along different gradients of the road, through different weather and varying temperatures. Augustine Baker makes no bones about that: 'The whole course of a spiritual life consists of perpetual changes, of elevations and depressions, and an extraordinary consolation is usually attended by succeeding anguish and desertion.' He goes on: 'Our supreme happiness is not receiving but giving; all these favours, therefore, and all these sufferings do end in this; namely, the accomplishment of this love in our souls, so that all our perfection consists in a state of love and an entire conformity with the divine will.'

The only thing to do, if we are going to complete this journey, is to plod on, to go on and to keep on going, up hill and down hill, through sunshine and rain, to persevere. Towards the end of the second volume of her autobiography, Maya Angelou, the black American writer, has a significant sentence which stresses the need to *practise* the virtue of perseverance (which she calls 'fortitude') every single day. 'Unfortunately, fortitude was not like the colour of my skin, given to me once and mine forever. It needed to be resurrected each morning and exercised painstakingly.'

Prayer is saying 'Yes' to God in faith and love. 'Perseverance', said Dr Somerset-Ward, 'is the surest sign of love.'

Shakespeare's Macbeth was not an heroic character. He was a brave, sensitive, vulnerable man who was destroyed by ambition. His life was a tragedy. Yet towards the end of the play, Shakespeare gave him his moment of glory. The glory of perseverance. His wife has died. Burnham Wood *has* come to Dunsinane. In one of his speeches, he swings between despair and perseverance. But perseverance wins.

I 'gin to be aweary of the sun,
And wish the estate o' the world were now undone.
Ring the alarum-bell! – Blow, wind! come, wrack!
At least we'll die with harness on our back.

What about the end of our journey? The point of arrival? It is the vision of God. God who is All-Beauty, All-Goodness, All-Truth, All-Love. It is to know God and to love him and to enjoy him for ever.

That, of course, is in heaven. That is where our journey ends. But here and now we are journeying towards it, preparing ourselves for it, putting ourselves in the way of it, perhaps even having a tiny foretaste of it now and then.

And this is where I say Good-bye. God be with you on your journey and give you grace to persevere.

13

Postscript

Corporate prayer

This book has been all about personal prayer. But perhaps I ought to add a postscript about corporate prayer, prayer with other people. Because we are not just separate individuals. We are members of a community. And so our prayer, like everything else, has a social context.

If we are Christians, we are not just individual Christians. We are members of the Christian community, members of the Church. And so, as well as our own personal communication with God, we should also join with other people in offering to God the prayer of the Church, the prayer of the body. This is what is meant by corporate prayer.

In order that it may be the prayer of the community, corporate prayer has a common form in which we all share. It is ordered and structured, like a symphony, a ballet or a drama and offered to God for his praise and glory.

Corporate prayer is offered to God in response to his love and power revealed in history. That is the purpose of the church calendar. It records the mighty acts of God, providing us with a programme for our worship – Christmas, Palm Sunday, Good Friday, Easter Day, Pentecost, and the weeks before and after, together with remembrances of the great heroes and heroines of the Church whom we call the saints.

The chief act of corporate worship is the Eucharist. I write as an Anglican, but this is true for Roman Catholics, members of the Orthodox Church – and indeed for many of the Free Churches.

The Eucharist is a great mystery. It is called by various names – the Mass, the Liturgy, the Holy Communion, the Holy

Mysteries, the Lord's Supper. It is 'the Lord's own service' instituted by Jesus in the upper room in Jerusalem on the night on which he was betrayed. It has been celebrated all down the ages ever since the resurrection, when the early Church met for 'the breaking of bread and the prayers' on the first day of the week, the resurrection day.

The Eucharist is a sacred meal. Bread and wine are offered to God upon the altar. Then they are consecrated, blessed by the Holy Spirit and set apart. They become sacramentally the Body and Blood of Christ. That is what they signify. They are the focal point of his Presence and Life. At the moment of communion, we eat and drink that bread and wine which represent the Body (Presence) and Blood (Life) of Christ. And in that act of eating and drinking, we are united with Christ and he with us.

We are also united with each other as members of his Body, the Church. For we kneel shoulder to shoulder, share the same bread and drink from the same cup. That act of communion which unites us to Christ unites us to each other. The Eucharist is a great love-feast, celebrating the love of God and the love of our fellow Christians.

Before the bread and wine is laid on the altar at the Offertory, there is a general confession of our sins, a particular prayer for the day called the collect, readings from the Bible and prayers of intercession. The great eucharistic prayer begins with the adoration of God, the sanctus ('Holy, holy, holy'), and the communion is followed by a prayer of thanksgiving and the blessing. Then we go out into the world 'to love and serve the Lord'. That is roughly the form of the service.

You may feel that I have painted it in rather romantic colours, (symphony, ballet, drama) and that your experience of corporate worship doesn't quite live up to that picture! Nevertheless, that is what it should be like. How can we make it so? The answer perhaps lies in our preparation for the Eucharist. We should not just drift in to church empty-handed. We should bring with us bits and pieces of prayer and worship which we have collected and put them into the common pool.

This is called Preparation for Communion. It need not take

very long. We could do it the day or the night before as part of our personal prayer. For example, ask yourself:

What particular sins am I aware of this week which I am going to put into that great stream of confession which goes up to God to receive his forgiveness?

What particular person or situation in the world am I going to remember in the intercession?

What particular thing am I going to offer to God with the bread and wine at the Offertory? It is a help, perhaps, to think of the bread as a symbol of our work and the wine as a symbol of our relationships.

What particular things am I going to be thankful for in the eucharistic prayer?

What particular thing about God am I specially going to worship and adore at the moment of the Sanctus?

What particular grace and help in my life do I desire at the moment of communion?

This preparation for the Eucharist is the bridge between personal prayer and corporate prayer. It means that we are making some contribution to the prayer of the body, putting something into it. It also means that we go to the service expectantly. And all this mysteriously affects the atmosphere of the service and indeed of the church building. It gives it a warmth and a sense of reality which affects other people.

People who pray vocally don't have much trouble with corporate worship. They are used to praying in words. People who pray mentally can probably get something out of the readings and – if they are lucky – the sermon. And also out of the ordered rhythm of the service and the words of the prayers.

It is people who pray silently, contemplatively, who have the greatest difficulty. It is a pity that there is not more silence in our corporate worship – after the readings and the sermon and certainly after the eucharistic prayer. There is provision for this in the new services, if only it were taken advantage of. But perhaps it is good for those of us who pray silently to have, for one hour a week, to pray vocally and mentally with our fellow human beings. It will keep our spirituality balanced and earthed. I'm sure that Baron von Hügel would agree! More-over, contemplatives ought to read these words of Kenneth Leech from the chapter on The Eucharistic God in his book *True God*: 'Holy Communion is the supreme mystical experi-ence, the heart of Christian contemplation, the climax of the life of prayer. It is a common act and yet at the same time deeply, intensely personal. Through this essentially material, physical activity, there is a participation in the being of God, a true union of the divine and human realms.'

We should not make corporate prayer more difficult than it need be. We are all made differently. Ought we not to respect that fact in our corporate worship as we do in our personal prayer? Some people like music, colour, movement in worship – even 'bells and smells'! Other people prefer a rather simpler form of service. Well, why not follow your particular 'attrait'? Why not adapt Dom John Chapman's famous dictum about prayer and apply it to your corporate worship – 'worship as you can and not as you can't'?

By the way, if you take your children to church with you and there is no creche provided, do see that they are well-provided with books to read, books to draw in, a supply of pencils or crayons and a favourite soft toy. And don't worry about them, fuss over them and fence them in. Children should go to church with their parents. But they *are* children and children are bound to be restless and make some noise. I hope that you have a congregation which accepts and welcomes children. Most congregations do. And when you go up to the altar to make your communion, take the children with you to receive a blessing. Above all, make corporate worship for your children a happy experience which they will remember.

One final point. Go out of your way to be friendly, warm and welcoming to other members of the congregation. We are a Christian family in corporate worhsip and we should try to behave like one. We are so bad about this in England. If we were in Africa, we should be dancing together in the aisle!

Some Classic Books of Spiritual Reading

George Appleton, *Journey for a Soul*, Collins Fontana Books 1974.

The Art of Prayer – An Orthodox Anthology, Faber & Faber 1966.

St Augustine, *Confessions*, Sheed & Ward 1943.

Augustine Baker, *Holy Wisdom*, Anthony Clarke Books 1964.

Anthony Bloom, *Living Prayer*, Darton Longman & Todd 1966.

Anthony Bloom, *School for Prayer*, Darton Longman & Todd 1970.

Dietrich Bonhoeffer, *Letters and Papers from Prison*, Collins Fontana Books 1959.

Jean-Pierre de Caussade, *Abandonment to Divine Providence*, Catholic Records Press 1921.

Dom John Chapman, *Spiritual Letters*, Sheed & Ward 1944.

The Cloud of Unknowing, Penguin Classics 1961.

Alan Ecclestone, *Yes to God*, Darton Longman & Todd 1975.

Enfolded in Love (Daily Readings with Julian of Norwich), Darton, Longman & Todd 1980.

James Finley, *Merton's Palace of Nowhere*, Ave Maria Press 1978.

Jean-Nicolas Grou, *The Hidden Life of the Soul*, Longmans 1907.

Walter Hilton, *The Ladder of Perfection*, Penguin Classics 1957.

Julian of Norwich, *Revelations of Divine Love*, Penguin Classics 1966.

Søren Kierkegaard, *Christian Discourses* (translated, with an

Introduction, by Walter Lowrie), Princeton University Press 1971.

Lamps of Fire (Daily Readings with St John of the Cross), Darton Longman & Todd 1985.

Kenneth Leech, *True God*, Sheldon Press 1985.

Kenneth Leech, *True Prayer*, Sheldon Press 1980.

Living Water (Daily Readings with St Teresa of Avila), Darton Longman & Todd 1985.

Andrew Louth, *The Origins of the Christian Mystical Tradition*, Clarendon Press 1981.

Thomas Merton, *Asian Journal*, Sheldon Press 1974.

Thomas Merton, *Conjectures of a Guilty Bystander*, Sheldon Press 1977.

Thomas Merton, *No Man is an Island*, Burns & Oates 1955.

Thomas Merton, *Thoughts in Solitude*, Burns & Oates 1958.

Donald Nicholl, *Holiness*, Darton Longman & Todd 1981.

Henri Nouwen, *The Genesee Diary*, Image Books 1981.

Henri Nouwen, *Reaching Out*, Collins Fount Paperbacks 1980.

Michael Ramsey, *Be Still and Know*, Collins Fount Paperbacks 1982.

Abbé de Tourville, *Letters of Direction*, Dacre Press 1939.

Evelyn Underhill, *The Fruits of the Spirit*, Longmans 1942.

W. H. Vanstone, *Love's Endeavour, Love's Expense*, Darton Longman & Todd 1977.

Baron von Hügel, *Spiritual Counsels and Letters*, Darton Longman & Todd 1964.

The Way, St. Christopher Press 1934 (by A Priest); *Following the Way*, SPCK 1958, and *To Jerusalem*, St. Christopher Press 1931 (both by the author of *The Way*) – three books by Dr Reginald Somerset-Ward which were published anonymously.

H. A. Williams, *The Joy of God*, Mitchell Beazley 1979.

H. A. Williams, *Tensions*, Mitchell Beazley 1976.

H. A. Williams, *True Resurrection*, Mitchell Beazley 1972.